HOW THE WORLD MAKES MUSIC

STRINGED INSTRUMENTS
by ANITA GANERI

A+
Smart Apple Media

Published by Smart Apple Media
P.O. Box 3263, Mankato, Minnesota 56002

Printed in the United States of America at Corporate Graphics, in North Mankato, Minnesota.

Library of Congress Cataloging-in-Publication Data
Ganeri, Anita, 1961-
 Stringed instruments / by Anita Ganeri.
     p. cm. — (How the world makes music)
 Includes index.
 Summary: "Describes various stringed instruments from around the world including familiar
instruments such as the guitar and violin, along with other traditional instruments such as the
Japanese Koto and Indian lutes"—Provided by publisher.
 ISBN 978-1-59920-480-2 (library binding)
 1. Stringed instruments—Juvenile literature. I. Title.
 ML750.G36 2012
 787'.19--dc22

                                                                                2010042418

Created by Appleseed Editions, Ltd.
Designed by Guy Callaby
Illustrated by Graham Rosewarne
Edited by Jinny Johnson
Picture research by Su Alexander

Picture credits:
l = left, r = right, t = top, b = bottom
Title page (left to right) Lebrecht Music & Arts Photo Library/Alamy, Adrian Sherratt/Alamy, Eye Ubiquitous/Alamy, Martin
Harvey/Alamy; contents page Denis Pepin/Shutterstock; Page 4 Brian A Jackson/Shutterstock; 5 Barone Firenze/Shutterstock; 6
Xavier Gallego Morell/Shutterstock; 7 Seow Yen Choon Kelvin/Shutterstock; 8 Denis Pepin/Shutterstock; 9 Aija Lehtonen/
Shutterstock; 10 Danita Delimont/Alamy; 11 Eye Ubiquitous/Alamy; 12 Vladimir Wrangel/Shutterstock; 13t Shishov Mikhail/
Shutterstock, b Route66/Shutterstock; 14 The Print Collector/Alamy; 15 Alaettin Yildirim/Shutterstock; 16 Imagebroker/Alamy;
17 Lebrecht Music & Arts Photo Library/Alamy; 18 Martin Harvey/Alamy; 19 Thefinalmiracle/Shutterstock; 20 Imagebroker/
Alamy; 21 Andreas Gradin/Shutterstock; 22 Adrian Sherratt/Alamy; 23 Karla Caspari/Shutterstock; 24 David Kilpatrick/Alamy;
25 Louise Batalla Duran/Alamy; 26 Angela N Hunt/Shutterstock; 27 Japan Art Collection (JAC)/Alamy; 28 Joe Kuchaski/
Shutterstock; 29 Pierre Brye/Alamy.
Front cover: Main pic – girl playing violin, Shutterstock; Grayscale b/g pic of harpist's hands, John Wollwerth/Shutterstock; Koto
players, Angela N Hunt/Shutterstock; Dulcimer player, Joe Kuchaski/Shutterstock; Lute player, Alaettin Yildirim/Shutterstock;
Rock guitarist, Andreas Gradin/Shutterstock

DAD0047
3-2011

9 8 7 6 5 4 3 2 1

Contents

Stringed Instruments

People all over the world make music. They play musical instruments and sing songs to express their emotions, and it's part of celebrations and other ceremonies. People enjoy listening to music as they go about their daily lives.

Vibrating Strings

There are many different types of musical instruments. This book is about instruments that have strings. Think about what happens if you stretch a rubber band tight, then twang it. You hear a humming noise. This is the sound made by the band as it moves, or vibrates, back and forth. The strings on instruments work in the same way. They are stretched tight, and they sound when they vibrate. Most instruments have a hollow body, which picks up the vibrations of the strings and makes them louder.

The guitar is a stringed instrument. The player makes the strings vibrate by plucking them with the fingers of the right hand.

In this picture of an orchestra, you can see two different kinds of stringed instruments, violas (on the left) and cellos (on the right).

Musical Notes

Some of the earliest stringed instruments were musical bows. These simple instruments were like the bows used for shooting arrows. They had one string, which was fastened to either end of a flexible stick and stretched tight.

Hollow gourd makes the sound louder

String

Flexible stick

The Violin Family

The violin is probably the best-known stringed instrument in Western music. The player holds the violin under the chin. It has four strings, which are played by moving a bow across them. The bow is a wooden stick with horse hair stretched from end to end. As the bow moves across the strings, it makes them vibrate.

The strings on a violin are tuned to four notes: G (below middle C), D, A, and E. The violinist uses the fingers of her left hand to play the notes in between.

In the Orchestra

The violin has a whole family of its own. Its members are the violin, viola, cello, and double bass. Together, these four instruments make up the string section of an orchestra. The viola is slightly larger than the violin, but it is held and played in the same way.

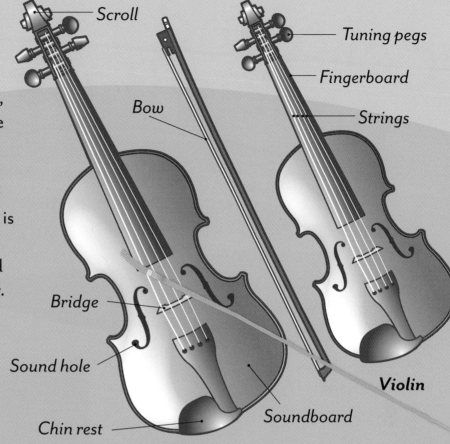

Scroll

Bow

Tuning pegs

Fingerboard

Strings

Bridge

Sound hole

Soundboard

Violin

Chin rest

Viola

Musical Notes

The bows that are used to play the violin, viola, cello, and double bass are usually threaded with hair from a horse's tail. There are about 150 hairs in a bow.

Cello and Double Bass

The cello and double bass are much bigger than the violin and viola. They have long strings, which play some very low notes. They are the bass section of the violin family. The cello also has a beautiful singing tone, which makes it a very popular instrument.

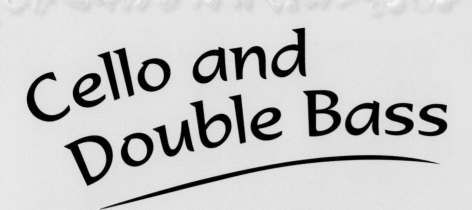

The cello is often played as a solo (on its own) instrument. Its large body gives it a rich, expressive sound.

Sitting and Standing

A cello player sits on a chair and rests the cello between the knees. There is a metal spike at the bottom to balance the cello on the floor. The double bass is huge! It measures about 6.2 feet (1.9 m) from its metal spike to the scroll at the top. It is so big that players perch on high stools or stand up to play it.

The double bass is often played in jazz music. Jazz players usually pluck the strings (above).

Musical Notes

The cello is played with a bow, but the double bass can be played with a bow or by plucking strings with the fingers.

Cello

Double Bass

Scroll

Bow

Fingerboard

Strings

Bridge

Spike

Folk Fiddle

In many countries, people use violins to play folk music. These violins are usually known as fiddles. One example comes from Hardanger, in Norway. Hardanger fiddles are often played to accompany dancing. They are beautifully decorated, with black ink patterns that are drawn on the wood.

This Hardanger fiddle has decorations made from mother-of-pearl along the fingerboard, and ink patterns on the soundboard.

Playing a Fiddle

The Hardanger fiddle has eight strings. Only four of them are actually played. The other four are called sympathetic strings because they vibrate "in sympathy" when the other strings are played, making a pleasant buzzing noise.

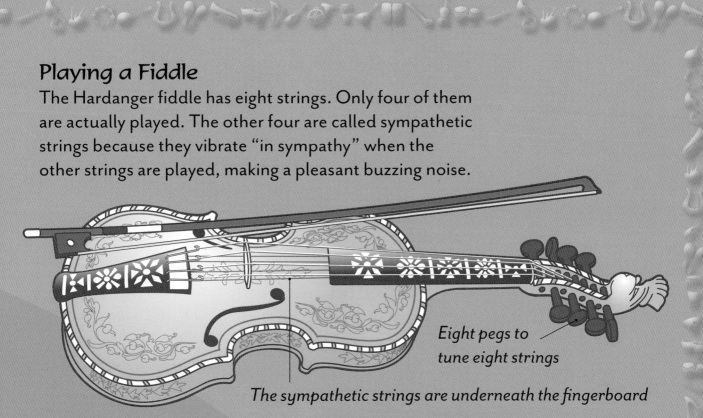

Eight pegs to tune eight strings

The sympathetic strings are underneath the fingerboard

Musical Notes

Some fiddles are very simple instruments. The imzad has only one string. It is played by the Tuareg people, who live in the Sahara Desert in northern Africa. The body of the imzad is often made from a large, hollow fruit, called a gourd. The imzad is used to accompany songs.

Harp

The harp is a very old instrument. Harps were played thousands of years ago in ancient Egypt and ancient Greece. A harp has lots of strings, which are stretched between a neck and a hollow sound box. Each string sounds a different note when it is plucked.

This ancient stone carving comes from Karnak in Egypt. It shows a musician playing a harp.

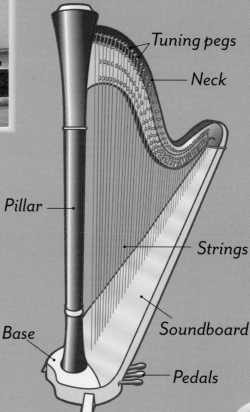

Orchestral Harp

The modern harp is played in orchestras. It has 47 strings, which are all tuned (tightened or loosened) to sound different notes. The harpist plays with a hand on either side of the strings. There are also pedals, which can be pressed down to shorten or lengthen all of the strings.

This harpist is "damping" the strings with her hands to stop them from sounding.

Tuning pegs

Neck

Pillar

Strings

Base

Soundboard

Pedals

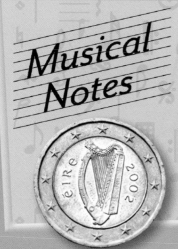

Musical Notes

The harp is the national instrument of both Ireland and Wales. The folk, or Celtic, harp appears on all of the coins used in Ireland.

Lute

The lute, like the harp, is an ancient instrument. There are paintings in ancient Egyptian tombs of people playing lutes. Today, there are many different kinds of lutes played all over the world. A lute has a sound box with a rounded back. The strings run across the sound box and along a thin neck.

This picture of an angel playing a lute is by the Italian artist Leonardo da Vinci. It was painted in the 1490s.

Playing a Lute

The player plucks the strings with one hand. The fingers of the other hand press the strings against the neck of the lute. This changes the length of the strings, so that the player can sound different notes. The longer the string, the deeper the note. For higher notes, the player shortens the string.

This modern lute is similar to the one in Leonardo da Vinci's painting. The peg box, the part that holds the tuning pegs, is bent at a right angle to the neck.

Musical Notes

Some lutes have lots of strings. All the strings have to be tuned so that they sound the correct notes before the player can start. With up to 24 strings to get right, this can take a long time!

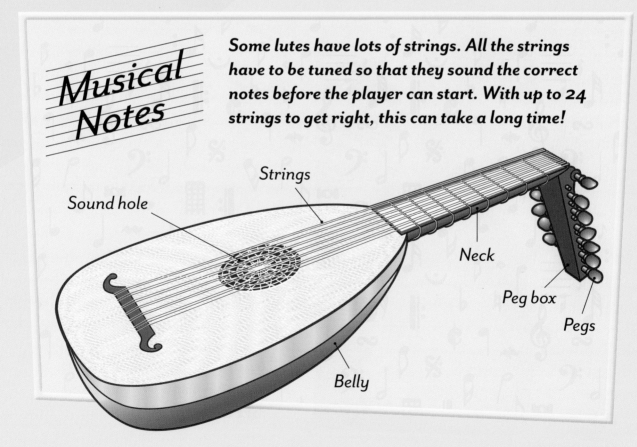

Strings

Sound hole

Neck

Peg box

Pegs

Belly

Shamisen

The shamisen is a kind of lute that is played in Japan. It has three strings, which were traditionally made from silk. The body is covered with animal skin, often from a cat. It is played by plucking the strings with a large plectrum—a flat piece of bone or shell.

A Japanese woman plays a shamisen, using a plectrum in her right hand.

Shamisen

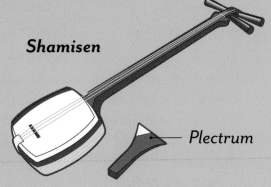

Plectrum

Musical Notes

The shamisen is played in lots of different kinds of music in Japan. It accompanies traditional Kabuki theater. It is also popular with some jazz and pop musicians.

The balalaika is a Russian instrument. It has a triangular-shaped body and usually three strings. There are many different sizes of balalaika, from the giant contrabass to the prima. The whole family of balalaikas is played together in orchestras.

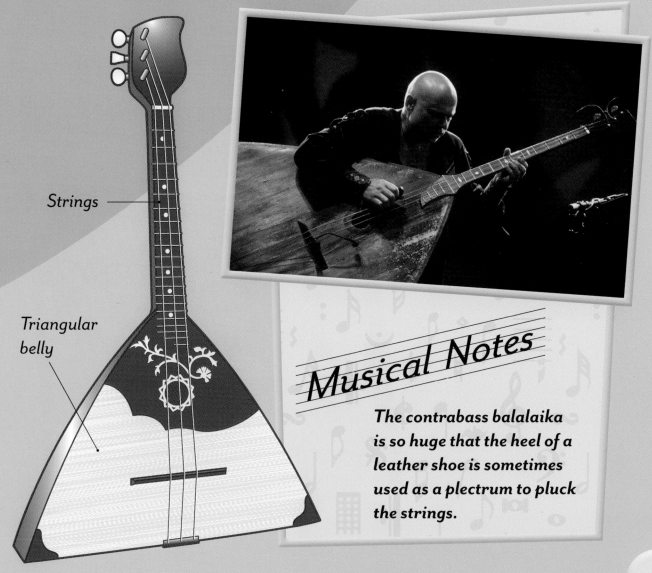

Strings

Triangular belly

Musical Notes

The contrabass balalaika is so huge that the heel of a leather shoe is sometimes used as a plectrum to pluck the strings.

Indian Lutes

The sitar and tambura are both types of lutes that are important in Indian music. The sitar has a wooden body and long neck. Seven strings run across arched metal supports that are tied onto the neck. These supports are called frets. There are up to 15 more strings beneath the frets. These are the sympathetic strings. They vibrate as the sitar is being played to give a beautiful, shimmering sound.

Indian musician Krishna Mohan Bhatt performs on his sitar. Sitar musicians usually sit on the floor to play.

Tambura

The tambura accompanies the beautiful melodies being played on the sitar. It does not have any frets. The player plucks the four metal strings one after the other in a regular pattern. This type of accompaniment is called a drone.

The tambura has a bridge that can be moved up and down to change the pitch of the notes.

Musical Notes

The most famous sitar player worldwide is Ravi Shankar. He worked with George Harrison of the Beatles, who introduced the sitar into pop music.

Metal frets

Tumba (resonator)

Sympathetic strings beneath frets

Sound box

Guitar

The guitar is one of the most popular of all the stringed instruments. There are two main kinds of guitar. The acoustic guitar has a hollow wooden body and a neck with metal frets. The sound of the strings vibrating is made louder by the hollow sound box. The electric guitar has a solid body. It uses an electric amplifier to pick up the strings' vibrations.

A man plays flamenco on an acoustic guitar at a concert in Spain.

Flamenco Guitar

The guitar originally came from Spain. Today, guitars are still used to accompany Spanish flamenco dancing. This exciting spectacle includes lots of foot stomping, hand clapping, and singing.

Musical Notes

In pop music, there are often two kinds of electric guitar working together. A bass guitar provides the chords and the beat of the music, while a lead guitar plays the melodies and solos.

Pegs

Strings

Frets

Fingerboard

Sound hole

Body

Bridge

Acoustic Guitar

Strap button

Neck

Pickups

Controls

Strap button

Electric Guitar

Ukelele

The ukelele was originally a kind of small Portuguese guitar. In the 1870s, it was taken by Portuguese settlers to Hawaii, in the Pacific Ocean, where it got its name. It quickly became very popular in Hawaii and in the United States.

Children at a school in Wales learn to play their ukeleles.

Banjo

The banjo has a round body made from a wooden frame covered with a skin, or plastic, and a long neck. It was developed by African slaves who were forced to work in the plantations of North America. They made instruments similar to the ones they had known at home in West Africa.

A banjo player in the Medicine Show Music Company performs at the Minnesota State Fair.

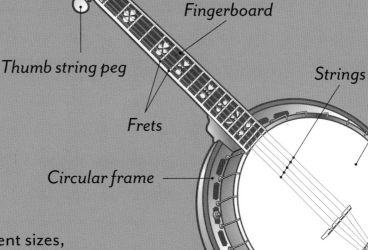

Thumb string peg

Fingerboard

Frets

Circular frame

Strings

Head

Banjo

Different Sizes

The banjo comes in different sizes, and can have four or five strings. Some players pluck the strings with their fingers. Others use a pick.

Zither

A zither is an instrument that has strings running along the entire length of its body. The strings are plucked with the fingers. In Africa, the simplest zithers are made by digging a shallow pit and stretching strings over the top. The pit acts as a kind of sound box. Other zithers are made by hollowing out a piece of wood, then stretching the strings across.

A musician plays a type of board zither from Greece. He plucks the strings with two small metal plectrums. These are called picks.

Sound hole

Accompanying strings

Tuning pegs

Melody strings

Frets

Modern Zither

Vina

The vina is an instrument from India. It is made from a long, hollow tube attached to two gourds. The strings run along the top of the tube. The tube and the gourds are the sound boxes that make the sound of the strings louder. Vinas are often beautifully decorated.

Musical Notes

In southern India, there is a slightly different type of vina, often known as the Saraswati vina. Saraswati is the Hindu goddess of learning. She is sometimes shown in pictures playing the vina.

Koto

The koto is a long wooden box that has a hole carved out underneath. On top, there are 13 strings, stretched from one end of the instrument to the other. The player wears three plectrums, which are attached to the thumb and first two fingers of the right hand. These plectrums are used to pluck the strings.

Koto players performing at the Meiji Jingu shrine in Tokyo, Japan. The koto is the national instrument of Japan.

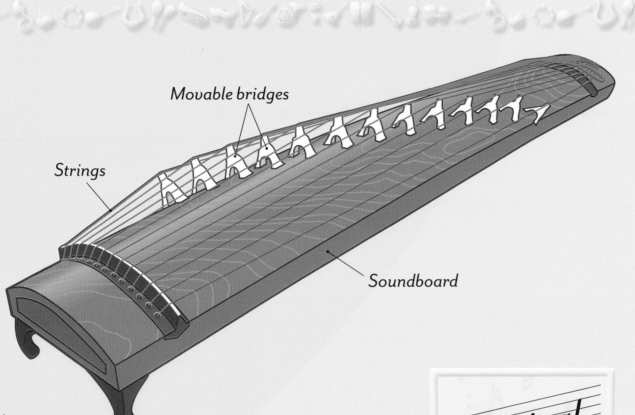

Movable bridges

Strings

Soundboard

Elegant Music

In the past, the koto was an important instrument in Gagaku music. This was the elegant music that was played only in the court of the Japanese emperor. Today, the koto is used in all kinds of music.

This portrait of a lady in traditional Japanese dress playing the koto was painted in the 1870s.

Musical Notes

The Tale of the Genji is a famous story written by a Japanese noblewoman, called Murasaki Shikibu, about 1,000 years ago. In it, Prince Genji falls deeply in love with a woman he has never seen after hearing her play on the koto.

Dulcimer

A dulcimer looks like a zither, but the player strikes the strings with hammers instead of plucking them with the fingers.

Cimbalom

The cimbalom is a kind of dulcimer. It is very popular in Hungary and other eastern European countries. The player uses two hammers to strike the instrument's metal strings. Some cimbaloms are quite small and are held by a strap that goes around the player's neck. There are also large cimbaloms that are built for concerts. Sometimes, the cimbalom plays in an orchestra.

The strings on this cimbalom run from side to side across two bridges.

Musical Notes

In Iran, the dulcimer is called the santur. Its 72 strings are played with two delicate wooden hammers.

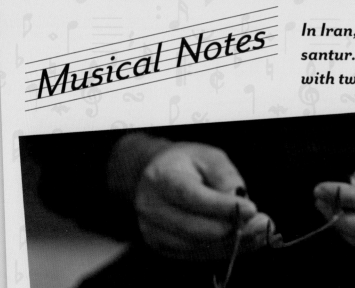

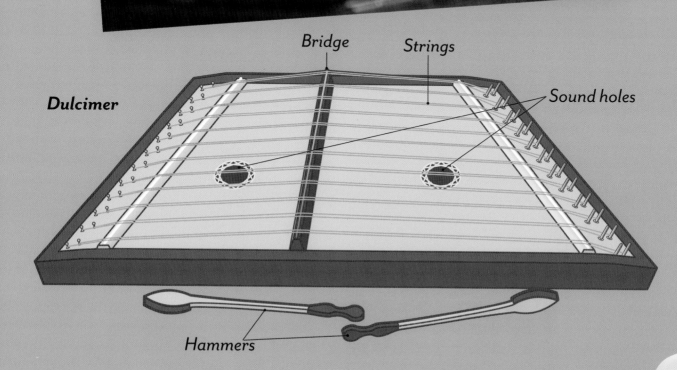

Dulcimer

Bridge

Strings

Sound holes

Hammers

Words to Remember

amplifier
an electric device that increases the volume of an instrument

bridge
a device on a stringed instrument that holds the strings away from the body of the instrument

drone
an accompaniment that remains at the same pitch, or group of pitches, throughout a piece of music

fingerboard
the part of a stringed instrument where the player presses the fingers down to change the length of a vibrating string, and therefore change the pitch

fret
a metal strip that runs across a fingerboard

gourd
a type of fruit with a thick skin; gourds can be hollowed out and dried to make musical instruments.

peg
a device used to tune the strings of a stringed instrument by loosening or tightening them

pickup
a device on an electric guitar that picks up the vibrations of the strings and converts them into electrical signals

pitch
how high or low a note is

plectrum

a piece of plastic, wood, shell, or similar hard material that is held in the fingers and used to pluck a string; also called a pick

pluck

If you pluck a string, you pull it sharply with your fingers, then let go so that the string vibrates.

soundboard

the part of a stringed instrument that picks up the vibrations of the strings and then transfers them to the surrounding air

sound box

the hollow part of a stringed instrument that makes the sound of the strings louder and gives the instrument its characteristic sound

sympathetic strings

strings that aren't played, but vibrate "in sympathy" as the melody strings are played; the sympathetic strings make a humming or buzzing sound.

tune

To tune a string means to tighten or loosen it until it sounds the required pitch.

vibrate

to move back and forth

Web Sites

Make A String Instrument!
http://www.dsokids.com/athome/instruments/string.aspx

Oregon Symphony Orchestra: The String Family
http://www.orsymphony.org/edu/instruments/strings.aspx

Sphinx Kids! Instrument Storage Room
http://www.sphinxkids.org/Instrument_Storage.html

String Instruments from China
http://www.philmultic.com/home/instruments/

Index